ISBN 0-590-06577-7

12 11 10 9 8 7 6 5 4 3 2 1   7 8 9/9 0 1 2/0

Printed in the U.S.A.   08

First Scholastic printing, January 1997

THE LITTLE BOOK OF

DOGS

Selected by Caroline Walsh

A TRUMPET CLUB SPECIAL EDITION

Contents

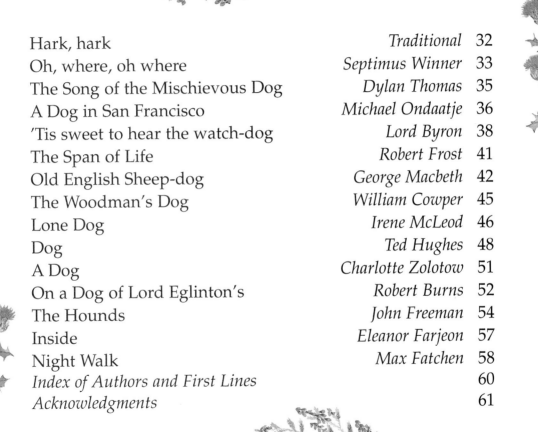

The Dog

The truth I do not stretch or shove
When I state the dog is full of love.
I've also proved, by actual test,
A wet dog is the lovingest.

OGDEN NASH

TO MY DOG

This gentle beast
This golden beast
laid her long chin
along my wrist

and my wrist
is branded
with her love
and trust

and the slat of my cheek
is hers to lick
so long as I
or she shall last

ADRIAN MITCHELL

11

DOGS AND WEATHER

I'd like a different dog
    For every kind of weather—
A narrow greyhound for a fog,
    A wolfhound strange and white,
With a tail like a silver feather
    To run with in the night,
When snow is still, and winter stars are bright.

In the fall I'd like to see
  In answer to my whistle,
A golden spaniel look at me.
  But best of all for rain
A terrier, hairy as a thistle,
  To trot with fine disdain
Beside me down the soaked, sweet-smelling lane.

WINIFRED WELLES

Did you ever know Yap?
The best little dog
Who e'er sat on a lap
Or barked at a frog.
His eyes were like beads,
His tail like a mop,
And it waggled as if
It never would stop.
His hair was like silk
Of the glossiest sheen,
He always ate milk,
And once the cold cream.

SUSAN COOLIDGE

from *What Katy Did*

Now the man has a child
He knows all the names
of the local dogs.

KARAI SENRU

Under the willow
With a leaf stuck in his mouth
The puppy sleeps.

KOBAYASHI ISSA

17

DOGS

O little friend, your nose is ready; you sniff,
Asking for that expected walk,
(Your nostrils full of the happy rabbit-whiff)
And almost talk.

HAROLD MONRO

from "Dogs"

CHUMS

He sits and begs; he gives a paw;
　　He is, as you can see,
The finest dog you ever saw,
　　And he belongs to me.

ARTHUR GUITERMAN
from "Chums"

AN INTRODUCTION TO DOGS

Dogs are upright as a steeple
And much more loyal than people.

OGDEN NASH
from "An Introduction to Dogs"

Man and Dog

Who's this—alone with stone and sky?
It's only my old dog and I—
It's only him; it's only me;
Alone with stone and grass and tree.

What share we most—we two together?
Smells, and awareness of the weather.
What is it makes us more than dust?
My trust in him; in me his trust.

Here's anyhow one decent thing
That life to man and dog can bring;
One decent thing, remultiplied
Till earth's last dog and man have died.

SIEGFRIED SASSOON

Who nightly in his den does lie
That slumbers only with one eye
And barks if any thing stirs nigh
       My Rover

Who finds me out both far and near,
Tracing my footsteps every where
And when I whistle's sure to hear
       My Rover

Who will himself from day to day
Tend sheep so well when I'm away
As not to let one go astray
       My Rover

And who when I at dinner sit
In silence seems to beg a bit
Then wags his tail in thanks for it
      My Rover

And who to please me with a trick
Will carry in his mouth a stick
Or any thing that's not too thick
      My Rover

Nay I need not no further go
For everything in short that you
Can please me with thoult freely do
      My Rover

JOHN CLARE

from "My Rover"

GREEDY DOG

This dog will eat anything.

Apple cores and bacon fat,
Milk you poured out for the cat.
He likes the string that ties the roast
And relishes hot buttered toast.
Hide your chocolates! He's a thief,
He'll even eat your handkerchief.
And if you don't like sudden shocks,
Carefully conceal your socks.

24

Leave some soup without a lid,
And you'll wish you never did.
When you think he must be full,
You find him gobbling bits of wool,
Orange peel or paper bags,
Dusters and old cleaning rags.

This dog will eat anything,
Except for mushrooms and cucumber.

Now what is wrong with those, I wonder?

JAMES HURLEY

OUR DOG CHASING SWIFTS

A border collie has been bred to keep
Order among those wayward bleaters, sheep.
Ours, in a sheepless garden, vainly tries
To herd the screaming black sheep of the skies.

U.A. FANTHORPE

TOM'S LITTLE DOG

Tom told his dog called Tim to beg,
And up at once he sat,
His two clear amber eyes fixed fast,
His haunches on his mat.

Tom poised a lump of sugar on
His nose; then, "Trust!" says he;
Stiff as a guardsman sat his Tim;
Never a hair stirred he.

"Paid for!" says Tom; and in a trice
Up jerked that moist black nose;
A snap of teeth, a crunch, a munch,
And down the sugar goes!

WALTER DE LA MARE

My Dog, He is an Ugly Dog

My Dog, he is an ugly dog,
he's put together wrong,
his legs are much too short for him,
his ears are much too long.
My dog, he is a scruffy dog,
he's missing clumps of hair,
his face is quite ridiculous,
his tail is scarcely there.

My dog, he is a dingy dog,
his fur is full of fleas,
he sometimes smells like dirty socks,
he sometimes smells like cheese.
My dog, he is a noisy dog,
he's hardly ever still,
he barks at almost anything,
his voice is loud and shrill.

My dog he is a stupid dog,
his mind is slow and thick,
he's never learned to catch a ball,
he cannot fetch a stick.
My dog, he is a greedy dog,
he eats enough for three,
his belly bulges to the ground,
he is the dog for me.

JACK PRELUTSKY

Two little dogs
Sat by the fire
Over a fender of coal-dust;
Said one little dog
To the other little dog,
If you don't talk, why, I must.

Hark, hark,
The dogs do bark,
The beggars are coming to town;
Some in rags,
And some in tags,
And one in a velvet gown.

Oh where, oh where has my little dog gone?
Oh where, oh where can he be?
With his ears cut short and his tail cut long,
Oh where, oh where is he?

SEPTIMUS WINNER

THE SONG OF THE MISCHIEVOUS DOG

There are many who say that a dog has its day,
    And a cat has a number of lives;
There are others who think that a lobster is pink,
    And that bees never work in their hives.
There are fewer, of course, who insist that a horse
    Has a horn and two humps on its head,
And a fellow who jests that a mare can build nests
    Is as rare as a donkey that's red.
Yet in spite of all this, I have moments of bliss,
    For I cherish a passion for bones,
And though doubtful of biscuit, I'm willing to risk it,
    And I love to chase rabbits and stones.
But my greatest delight is to take a good bite
    At a calf that is plump and delicious;
And if I indulge in a bite at a bulge,
    Let's hope you won't think me too vicious.

DYLAN THOMAS

A Dog in San Francisco

Sitting in an empty house
with a dog from the Mexican circus!
O Daisy, embrace is my only pleasure.
Holding and hugging my friends.
Education.
A wave of eucalyptus. Warm granite.
These are the things I have in my heart.
Heart and skills, there's nothing else.

I usually don't like small dogs but you
like midwestern women take over the air.
You leap into the air and pivot
a diver going up! You are known
to open the fridge and eat when you wish.

36

I always wanted to be a dog
but I hesitated
for I thought they lacked certain skills.
Now I want to be a dog.

MICHAEL ONDAATJE

'Tis sweet to hear the watch-dog's honest bark
Bay deep-mouthed welcome as we draw near home;
'Tis sweet to know there is an eye will mark
Our coming, and look brighter when we come.

LORD BYRON

from "Don Juan"

THE SPAN OF LIFE

The old dog barks backward without getting up.
I can remember when he was a pup.

ROBERT FROST

Old English Sheep-dog

Eyes
drowned in fur:
an affectionate,

rough, cumulus
cloud, licking
wrists and

panting, fur
too hot
in your

"profuse" coat
of old wool. You
bundle yourself

about on
four shaggy
pillars

of Northumberland
lime-stone,
gathering sheep.

GEORGE MACBETH

THE WOODMAN'S DOG

Shaggy, and lean, and shrewd, with pointed ears,
And tail cropp'd short, half lurcher and half cur—
His dog attends him. Close behind his heel
Now creeps he slow; and now, with many a frisk
Wide-scampering, snatches up the drifted snow
With ivory teeth, or plows it with his snout;
Then shakes his powder'd coat, and barks with joy.

WILLIAM COWPER

Lone Dog

I'm a lean dog, a keen dog, a wild dog and lone,
I'm a rough dog, a tough dog, hunting on my own!
I'm a bad dog, a mad dog, teasing silly sheep;
I love to sit and bay the moon and keep fat souls from sleep.

I'll never be a lap dog, licking dirty feet,
A sleek dog, a meek dog, cringing for my meat.
Not for me the fireside, the well-filled plate.
But shut door and sharp stone and cuff and kick and hate.

Not for me the other dogs, running by my side,
Some have run a short while, but none of them would bide.
O mine is still the lone trail, the hard trail, the best,
Wide wind and wild stars and the hunger of the quest.

IRENE McLEOD

Dog

Asleep he wheezes at his ease.
He only wakes to scratch his fleas.

He hogs the fire, he bakes his head
As if it were a loaf of bread.

He's just a sack of snoring dog.
You can lug him like a log.

You can roll him with your foot.
He'll stay snoring where he's put.

Take him out for exercise
He'll roll in cowclap up to his eyes.

He will not race, he will not romp.
He saves his strength for gobble and chomp.

He'll work as hard as you could wish
Emptying the dinner dish.

Then flops flat, and digs down deep,
Like a miner, into sleep.

TED HUGHES

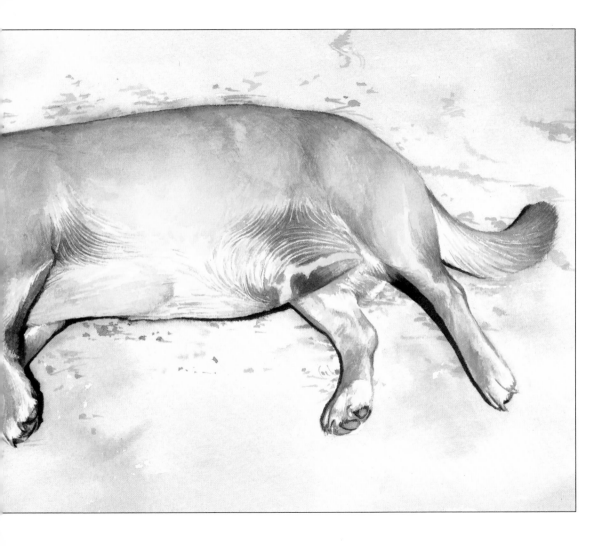

A Dog

I am alone.
Someone is raking leaves
outside
and there is one yellow leaf
on the black branch
brushing the window.
Suddenly a cold wet nose
nuzzles
my empty hand.

CHARLOTTE ZOLOTOW

On a Dog of Lord Eglinton's

I never barked when out of season,
I never bit without a reason;
I ne'er insulted weaker brother,
Nor wronged by force or fraud another.
We brutes are placed a rank below;
Happy for man could he say so.

ROBERT BURNS

THE HOUNDS

Far off a lonely hound
Telling his loneliness all round
To the dark woods, dark hills, and darker sea;

And, answering, the sound
Of that yet lonelier sea-hound
Telling his loneliness to the solitary stars.

Hearing, the kenneled hound
Some neighborhood and comfort found,
And slept beneath the comfortless high stars,

But that wild sea-hound
Unkenneled, called all night all round—
The unneighbored and uncomforted cold sea.

JOHN FREEMAN

INSIDE

A bellyful and the fire,
And him in his old suit,
And me with my heart's desire,
My head across his foot.

And I doze. And he reads.
And the clock ticks slow.
And, though he never heeds,
He knows, and I know.

Presently, without look,
His hand will feel to tug
My ear, his eyes on book,
Mine upon the rug.

ELEANOR FARJEON

Night Walk

What are you doing away up there
On your great long legs in the lonely air?
    Come down here, where the scents are sweet,
    Swirling around your great, wide feet.

How can you know of the urgent grass
And the whiff of the wind that will whisper and pass
    Or the lure of the dark of the garden hedge
    Or the trail of a cat on the road's black edge?

What are you doing away up there
On your great long legs in the lonely air?
    You miss so much at your great, great height
    When the ground is full of the smells of night.

Hurry then, quickly, and slacken my lead
For the mysteries speak and the messages speed
    With the talking stick and the stone's slow mirth
    That four feet find on the secret earth.

MAX FATCHEN

Index of Authors and First Lines

Acknowledgments

The publisher would like to thank the copyright holders for permission to reproduce the following copyright material:

Walter de la Mare: The Literary Trustees of Walter de la Mare and The Society of Authors as their representative for "Tom's Little Dog" from *The Complete Poems of Walter de la Mare* by Walter de la Mare. **U.A. Fanthorpe**: U.A. Fanthorpe for "Our Dog Chasing Swifts" copyright © U.A. Fanthorpe 1988. **Eleanor Farjeon**: David Higham Associates Ltd. for "Inside" from *Silver, Sand and Snow* by Eleanor Farjeon, Michael Joseph. **Max Fatchen**: John Johnson (Author's Agent) Ltd. for "Night Walk" from *Songs for My Dog and Other People* by Max Fatchen, Penguin Books Ltd. **Robert Frost**: Henry Holt & Co. Inc. for "The Span of Life" from *The Poetry of Robert Frost*, edited by Edward Connery Lathem copyright © Lesley Frost Ballantine 1964, copyright © Henry Holt & Co. Inc. 1969. **Arthur Guiterman**: Louise H. Sclove for "Chums" by Arthur Guiterman. **Ted Hughes**: HarperCollins Publishers Inc. for "Dog" from *What is the Truth?: A Farmyard Fable for the Young* by Ted Hughes, HarperCollins Inc. copyright © Ted Hughes 1984. **James Hurley**: James Hurley for "Greedy Dog" copyright © James Hurley 1973. **Kobayashi Issa**: John Murray (Publishers) Ltd. for the "Under the Willow" by Kobayashi Issa from *The Autumn Wind*, John Murray (Publishers) Ltd. **George MacBeth**: Sheil Land Associates Ltd. for "Old English Sheepdog" from *The Night Stones* by George MacBeth, Macmillan London Ltd. copyright © George MacBeth. **Adrian Mitchell**: Peters Fraser & Dunlop Group Ltd. for "To My Dog" from *The Ape Man Cometh* by Adrian Mitchell, Jonathan Cape Ltd. None of Adrian Mitchell's poems are to be used in any examination whatsoever. **Ogden Nash**: Little, Brown & Co. for "The Dog" from *Custard and Company* by Ogden Nash, Little, Brown & Co. 1980 copyright © Ogden Nash 1957, renewed by Frances Nash, Isabel Nash Eberstadt, and Linell Nash Smith 1985 and for the extract from "An Introduction to Dogs" from *The Face is Familiar* by Ogden Nash, Little, Brown & Co. **Michael Ondaatje**: Marion Boyars Publishers Ltd. for "A Dog in San Francisco" from *Secular Love* by Michael Ondaatje, Marion Boyars Publishers Ltd. **Jack Prelutsky**: William Morrow & Co. Inc. for "My Dog, He is an Ugly Dog" from *The New Kid on the Block* by Jack Prelutsky, William Morrow & Co. Inc. 1984 copyright © Jack Prelutsky 1984. **Siegfried Sassoon**: George Sassoon for "Man and Dog" by Siegfried Sassoon. **Karai Senru**: Penguin Books Ltd. for "Now the Man" by Karai Senru from *The Penguin Book of Japanese Verse*, translated by Geoffrey Brownas and Anthony Thwaite, Penguin Books 1964 copyright © Geoffrey Brownas and Anthony Thwaite 1964. **Dylan Thomas**: David Higham Associates Ltd. for "The Song of the Mischevious Dog" from *The Poems* by Dylan Thomas, J.M. Dent & Sons Ltd. copyright © Dylan Thomas.

Every effort has been made to obtain permission to reproduce copyright material but there may be cases where we have been unable to trace a copyright holder. The publisher will be happy to correct any omissions in future printings.